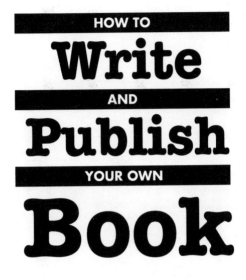

HOW TO
Write
AND
Publish
YOUR OWN
Book

HOW TO Write AND Publish YOUR OWN Book

By
Cuttie W. Bacon, III, Ph.D
Co-Author
Cuttie W. Bacon, IV, MBA

Published by:
Dr. Knose Publications
Chicago, Illinois

How to Write and Publish Your Own Book

By: Cuttie W. Bacon, III, Ph.D.
Co-authored by: Cuttie W. Bacon, IV

Copyright © MM

Published by Dr. Knose Publications, Chicago, Illinois

Cover Design and Page Layout by:
Ad Graphics, Inc., Tulsa, OK

Printed in the United States of America

ISBN Number: 0-9678544-0-7

Reasons why this book is a must for you

This book shows you:

1. How to start a book.

2. How to keep your writing simple.

3. How to reduce your fear of writing a book.

4. How to tape for a total of two hours and translate the tape into a 125 page book.

5. How to turn a speech into a book.

6. How to write 1,500 words per day or type two double-spaced sheets per day. In 15 days you will have a book.

7. How to dictate for 2 1/2 hours and have the dictation transcribed into a book.

8. How to self-publish your book.

9. How to promote your book.

There is no better time than now to write your book.

So write or type your first five pages NOW!

– Cuttie W. Bacon, III

You do not have to be a nuclear physicist to write a book

Most of my life, I've thought that in order to write a book one needed to be a genius and have a lot of degrees. Do not be deceived. You have all of the skills that are necessary to write a book. Writing a book requires you to sit down in a quiet place with a note pad or a typewriter and make a ten-chapter outline. You can also use a personal computer or tape recorder to dictate, or dictate to a secretary and accomplish the same result.

---

*You don't have to have
a printing company to
publish your book*

— Cuttie W. Bacon, III

You don't have to have a printing company to publish your book

There are several easy steps in publishing your book. First, type your manuscript or have it typed. After your manuscript is ready for publishing, contract the services of a book printing company. Usually 3,000 copies cost less than $5,000. Using the services of a professional graphic artist that knows how to communicate with a book printing company is all you need to self-publish your book. Many graphic artists are eagerly waiting to serve you and design your book cover. Numerous book-publishing companies are eager to contract with you to print your book. If you need recommendations of graphic artists and book printing companies, please call me or a staff member at 1-800-955-9934.

Foreword

Several years ago, after I completed my dissertation of more than 150 pages, and after bragging and showing it to my friends, it occurred to me that I should write a book on how to write your own book. But, because I am a great procrastinator, an outstanding innovator, and a very busy person, I never took the time to stop and pull my thoughts together and write. Since I never learned to type well, I was fearful of a personal computer until I sat down and typed three single-spaced pages and found that I had enough words to write the first chapter. It is now clear to me that this is the book for you to use as a guide to write your first book.

First, think of a title. It may be a temporary one, but the title will evolve as you write. Next, make your writing a speech—preferably a one-hour speech. If you choose, use a tape recorder and a one-hour tape. After you draft an outline for your one-hour speech, start talking. When you finish the tape, take it to a typist with a PC and have the typist put it on a floppy disk. If you do not know how to use a computer, have the typist print out a hard copy for you. You now have a rough draft of the first half of your book. Make corrections, rewrites, and do the same thing over again for the second half of your book. At this point, you should have at least nine pages.

Now you have a very rough draft of your book.

Congratulations!

Acknowledgments

I am grateful for the huge numbers of friends, relatives and acquaintances that encouraged me to write this book. On the first day I started writing, and mentioned to my friends what I was working on, they said to get started and told me they were convinced that I could complete a book on how to write a book. And a special thank you to my many friends in the National Association for African American speakers who read and listened to portions of the book before its publication. Also to my loving Mother who has never doubted any project I have undertaken from the time I was one day old up to this very day. I am deeply indebted to her for her constant support and encouragement.

Table of Contents

Introduction

This is how to write and publish a non-fiction book. I did not spend any time on fiction books because I am committed to writing and publishing non-fiction material.

How to Write and Publish Your Own Book is a combination of common sense and ordinary steps. I was motivated to do this because I rarely have conversations with individuals who believe their stories, their history, their accomplishments and their lives are documented in a fair and unbiased way. The purpose of this book is to serve as a vehicle for large numbers of people to write on topics about which they have a passion. Do not worry about the perfect book because perfection is not the goal. The goal is truth. After you use this book, please recommend it to others so that they may use the same technique to document their personal truths whether they are historical, anthropological, sociological or instructional. My only hope is that of the tens of thousands of individuals using this book, each will commit to doing his or her very best, for that is all that we can really ask of ourselves.

– Cuttie W. Bacon, III, Ph.D.

A related quote to begin each chapter will better clarify your idea.

– Cuttie W. Bacon, IV

CHAPTER 1

Choose a Subject

Uniqueness

Make your book different than any other. Ask yourself, "what is unique and different about my book that puts it in a class of its own?" List four distinctive things that set your book apart from all other books on the market.

Role Play

Have a friend pretend that he/she is a publisher. Give him/her four questions and ask them to allow you one minute to answer questions about the uniqueness and what distinguishes your book from all other books on the shelf. Have your friend role play that he/she is a bookstore owner and you convince them that they should stock a few hundred of your books in their store.

Write a 30-second advertisement for radio and for TV to persuade the listening and looking audience to buy your book.

Keep these questions in mind as you write your book and you will uniquely be able to distinguish your book from other books in the bookstore.

In choosing your subject you should focus on these objectives:

First, whatever subject you choose, you need to have experiences, expertise, and formal and/or informal experience in that area. Please do not misunderstand me. You do not need to be a world-renowned expert on the subject. You do need to be able to say, "I have a considerable amount of information, I know it well, and I know it well enough to stand up and talk about it for two hours. In addition to knowledge of the subject, you need a commitment to research the subject and a passion for sharing this information with many others.

You need a subject that is interesting. A subject like bird watching may not be interesting to a large number of people. All people would not want to read about it. Neither is Y2K. Y2K has come and gone and nothing came of it.

The subject should attract the interest of large numbers of people. A book like "Tuesdays with Maury" sold large numbers in two years primarily because it is about aging, life, and things we already know. Thus, it was very appealing to a large number of people. Keep in mind a paperback usually costs between $10 and $20. Make sure your topic will generate enough interest that people will spend $10 - $20 to have a copy of it. Remember women buy more than 75% of all trade books. Make sure your book appeals to that 75% of the population that usually purchases books.

My objective for writing this book was to re-create the fun, the challenge, the excitement, and the personal satisfaction I received in writing my first book. I was shocked when I finally completed it. I was puzzled as to why it took me so long to sit down and write my first book for publication. While I was writing the book, many people shared in my excitement and insisted that I make certain that they got a copy so they could use the examples and write their own book. I believe that any person that can read can use this book as a guideline to writing a book. I certainly hope that people of every age group will use this book as a guide. I only wish that I had taken the time to document all of the information and lessons that my grandmothers taught me. For several summers between the ages of 6 and 12 I lived with two grandmothers who always reassured me and treated me like a little prince. By the time I was 12 years old, no one could convince me that I was not of royal blood, because they both assured me that I was from royal blood on BOTH sides of my family. You,

---

*He who waits for tomorrow
forgets tomorrow never comes.*

Do it now.

– Cuttie W. Bacon, III

---

too, are of royal blood. You are princes, princesses, kings and queens of your destiny. With the mere utterance of your desires, you commit them to being. As we thinketh, so do we doeth. Don't just think about it, do it. As William Earnest Henley wrote in his poem *Invictus*, we are the masters of our fate, we are the captains of our souls . . . and our destinies!

I look forward to thousands of people writing and calling me, letting me know that they have used this book as a guide on writing their first book. I only hope that they will share each of their books with me. Nothing would please me more than to have one million authors use my book as a guide in writing their own book.

Something to spark you...

Your battery is already charged, but you can still jump-start your writing.

In writing your book, don't focus on profit. Focus on doing a good job. The profit will come.

— Cuttie W. Bacon, IV

CHAPTER 2

Investigating Your Subject and Collecting Data

Before you begin dictating or writing, spend at least 40 hours researching your subject area. It is crucial to know what other books have been written on the same subject. Review those books and know what they are saying and determine what will be unique about your book. Today, you can find book stores online such as, 'Barnes and Nobles' and 'Borders' to get a list of all books in print and many books that are out of print on a particular subject. Review the card file listing in your library. Look up the subjects or do a title search. Find the books on the shelves. Check them out and skim them. Make sure that you record information that you need for your book. Research newsletters and magazines on your subject. Check with your librarian for periodical directories and newsletter directories. Discuss your subject to get any suggested references and reading. I have found them to be very resourceful. Visit some larger bookstores and research books on your subject and inquire how they are selling. Get information from your research to use in your book. While you are researching in the bookstore, notice covers that look similar to what you would like your book to be as a final product. Buy one or two books like this and use them as a guide for putting your book together.

Keep in mind, as you do your research, to be careful of overkill. Statistics on how only 10% of the population in the United States reads books indicate that the majority of Americans do not complete them after they start reading them.

Attempting to put together a book with more than 200 pages is designing a book which will reach a limited number of people. Say what you have to say. Say all that you have to say. Keep it short and to the point.

You can significantly enhance the smoothness of writing your book by taking the data you have collected and the books and articles you have read and organizing your notes in a logical sequential order. For example, if you are writing a "How to Book," for example; "How to Stay Physically Fit 30 Days a Month," make certain that you organize your information. First in categories of eating, exercise, working, after work activities, sleeping, meditation, body massages, alcohol and tobacco consumption, various kinds of physical fitness programs, health clubs, participating sports, observation sports, high impact sports, low impact sports and consultation with a physician before starting.

Listing all the parts of the book that you intend to write about then organizing your list in some kind of sequential order will seriously aid you in deciding chapters and deciding what order you will write, dictate or record your information. It will enhance how smooth your writing activities go and how sequential your information is.

Right now, this minute is the best time to get started.

– Cuttie W. Bacon, IV

CHAPTER 3

Book Titles and Subtitles

Book titles and subtitles are crucial to selling a book. Look at your title and subtitle as the number one vehicle to sell your book. Keep in mind that an attractive title will give a good book the spark it needs to sell. Take your time and take an hour or two and carefully decide on a title and subtitle. Make 20 copies of your title and subtitle and pass them around to 20 people whose opinions you respect. Collect them after a week and examine them. Make revisions in your title if you feel the need to do so. After you make the changes, pass that title and subtitle to 10 people that you respect and see what you get. While you are revising, keep in mind your title should be easy to say and easy to remember. It should be short and should sell your book. Your subtitle is generally longer and gives more of a description. A subtitle should be able to separate your book from other books. As you know, book titles are so numerous they cannot be copyrighted. Go to the library or bookstore and look at dozens of titles and ask yourself what subtitles grab your attention quickly and what subtitles you think will help sell the book. Remember it is YOUR book. You can keep changing it until you get it right.

Ingredients of Excellent Titles

Invent new terminology:

- Y2K
- Cyberspace

Make outrageous promises:

- Spend more and have more money.
- Drive 100 miles an hour without risk.
- Drink a fifth of alcohol without getting intoxicated.

Make everyday statements:

- You do not have to be a rocket scientist.
- I never said I was perfect.

A title can also be a how to:

- How to play golf one hole at a time.
- How to ride a bike with no hands.
- How to paint a car with a silk screen.

Titles can also have unique combinations of words:

- Simple extravagance
- Flamboyant simplicity

- Arrogant modesty
- Obnoxiously loving

Ingredients of an excellent title:
- Hard to forget
- Unique
- Quickly state what the book is about
- Creates a desire to read
- Never negative

Resources to Develop Good Titles

Bring together a group of your friends and co-workers and ask each of them to write down five titles for your book. Get together a group of at least ten people and have them critique each chapter, then narrow it down to five people, then two.

Usually in an exploratory session like this, you can come up with an acceptable title. You may want to use a large pad to write down everybody's suggested titles. When you present each title, devise a rule that everybody states at least two good things about the title. After discussing each title, thank the group and take all the titles and try to come up with two that are very unique. This may assist you in coming up with the so called "perfect title." If you are not satisfied with what you come up with, have another exploratory session with ten different people and see what you come up with.

Don't wait.

Make haste.

Start writing at a fast pace.

– Cuttie W. Bacon, III

Example Title: Living Prosperously in the 21st Century

Example Subtitle: First Develop a Prosperity Consciousness

Example Chapters:

Chapter 1 – How to Get Rid of a Self Defeating Conscious

Chapter 2 – How to Get Rid of Poor Thinking

Chapter 3 – How to Think Rich

Chapter 4 – How to Stay Focused

Chapter 5 – How to Surround Yourself with Successful People

Chapter 6 – How to Meditate

Chapter 7 – How to Identify Your Birthright Wealth

Chapter 8 – Ten Daily Habits of Prosperous People

Chapter 9 – Make Long Term and Short Term Goals for Yourself to Acquire Prosperity

Chapter 10 – Twenty Ways to Stay Stimulated and Motivated Towards Your Goal

Chapter 11 – Conclusion

*A great challenge in writing
a book is to decide what's
important and disregard
what's not.*

– Cuttie W. Bacon, IV

CHAPTER 4

Designing Your Book Cover

Think about how you want to attract people to your book. Remember your book cover is the first impression of your content. How you design your book cover will have a significant effect on how your book sells. Using your computer is a great way to design your cover. Most software packages have a graphic section such as Windows 98 Powerpoint. Powerpoint gives you a huge number of options and graphic designs. You can cut and paste and add color. If you are not familiar with graphics, then sit with someone who is and tell them the colors you like and come up with fun cover designs.

After you experiment on the design of your book cover with some of the ideas I have mentioned, then locate a professional graphic artist who works with printing companies and understands how to communicate with print professionals. I recommend that you identify a professional graphic artist and look at samples of book covers so that you will be aware of the skills and talents of that particular artist. I would not select a heart surgeon who has only performed 1 or

2 operations, nor would I select a graphic artist who has only designed 1 or 2 book covers. I would not choose an artist who has designed only a few book covers because one of the things that will sell your book is the cover and the spine of your book. The design and the artwork, the colors, and the presentation are crucial in giving your book a professional appeal, a buying appeal and a successful look. The cost for a professional graphic artist to design a book cover varies. My experience has been that cover designs usually range somewhere between $500 – $2,000 dollars. In my opinion $1,500 – $2,000 is not too much for a professional to design a cover for your book.

Back Cover

The back cover is also a big selling point. Most shoppers are going to spend less than a minute reviewing the back cover of your book. This is a great opportunity to make it very clear the benefits of buying and reading your book. Remember you have possibly a minute or less to make a sales pitch that will send them to the cash register to purchase your book.

One of the most effective uses of a back cover is to tell the prospective buyers how the book may help him or why he should read the book. In my last book, *How to Teach Kids to Be Millionaires*, I used the back cover, first to say that my book was a clear, easy and simple method of teaching kids to accumulate wealth. Secondly, I wrote the following:

- Teach a child and a young adult how to never be broke, how to always pay oneself.

- How to grow money.

- How to be financially secure before 21.

- How to invest $1 - $2 per day.

- How to never use a credit card.

- How to earn your own money.

- How to spend your money wisely.

- How to invest for your children from birth to 21.

- How to tithe and how to give.

The back of the book can also be used to tell a little about the author and co-author. Another use of the back is to list what renowned writers, celebrities and people of high respect say about your book. Some of the quotes I am collecting for the revision of *How to Teach Kids to Be Millionaires* are as follows:

Noted CEO of a local bank says "*How to Teach Kids to be Millionaires* is a must reading for any adult who is involved with a child."

Local stock-broker says "*How to Teach Kids to Be Millionaires* should be required reading for all parents of young children."

National Radio talk host says *"How to Teach Kids to be Millionaires* is a clear, simple and useful guide for teaching kids how to manage money."

Noted college economics professor says "I wished I had this book 20 years ago when my son was 5 years old."

Front Cover

The front cover should have the title, subtitle and the author's name. You should avoid crowding your cover. Background colors should be bright and attractive. Your front cover should be easy to read and should make it impossible for a person not to pick it up when searching the shelves. Remember, in a bookstore your book is displayed on the shelf with only the spine visible. Your title should be easy to read at a glance so that when one is searching the shelves your title stands out, it is easily read, and will encourage one to take it out, look at it, and consequently buy it.

Remember the old saying that you can't tell a book by its cover? Keep in mind that statistics make it very clear that most people do not read the book they purchase. The most a person can tell by the book is its cover.

Getting Ready to Print Your Book

GET A GREAT GRAPHIC ARTIST

Get a graphic artist with extensive experience to help you design your book. Listen to the recommendations of your graphic artist. Try not to be too touchy about his/her recommendations. Generally they know what they are talking about. If you really want to make some changes after you print your first 10,000 copies, make the changes when you have a reprint. Talk to as many people as you can who have written a book and get their advice and recommendations.

No matter how small you believe your idea is, it is probably very big and exciting to someone else.

– Cuttie W. Bacon, IV

CHAPTER 5

Editing Your Manuscript

Once you have completed your manuscript, it is time for a 3-step editing process. Editing can be three of the most important steps of your book. These steps will take it from just a manuscript to a document ready for publishing.

The first and most important edit is the content edit. The content edit is when the book is checked for organization for a smooth flow and thought process, and for its basic organization.

The second step is the copy edit. The copy edit is where the grammar, punctuation, and spelling are corrected and put in proper form.

The third step is the design edit. This is where you arrange your charts and graphs to ensure your manuscript is in professional organizational form.

Because each of these three steps overlap you may find yourself involved in one or two of the editing steps at one time. Don't be concerned about steps overlapping. In my opinion, you cannot over-edit a manuscript.

Content Edit

A content edit will separate a professional book from an amateur book. Content edit is where a skilled editor makes sure the author's writing is well organized, that his thoughts and focus are coherent, and that his sentence structure paragraphs and thoughts are clear and well written. This is also a step where a book, if it hasn't been divided in chapters, is developed into its logical sequential chapters. It is also the step to determine that the book follows a logical sequence. The content edit makes sure that the subject matter is clear and that the ideas are focused and clearly written. If the organization of the book and ideas are not clearly focused, this is a stage that the author is advised to rewrite to make certain that the ideas and content are clear. A professional editor, when editing a manuscript, will make sure that the author's ideas and thought processes are precise. A professional editor's main focus is to improve the author's style and make certain his thoughts and points of view are very clear. At the content editing stage, most editors will read the manuscript 2 to 4 times focusing on a specific area each time;

- Making certain that the focus and the book is clear.

- Making certain that the organization of the book is orderly and flows smoothly.

- Making certain that the breakdown of the chapters is logical and sequential.

- Making certain that the book is professionally presented and has a potential of becoming a best seller.

Copy Edit

Copy editing is focused on grammar, sentence structure, word usage and spelling. This area is given very careful attention to detail and each sentence and paragraph is scrutinized to make certain the manuscript is professional in appearance. The copy edit step is also the time to focus on paragraph structure. If paragraphs are too long or choppy, this is the time to reduce them, which provides easy comprehension for the reader. Copy edit is also the step used to apply subheadings, to re-title chapters and subheads, and to improve the organization and the readability of the book. The higher degree of perfection that we master in the copy edit step will allow fewer changes and corrections once the book goes to the printer. After the book goes to the printer it becomes increasingly expensive to make changes and corrections.

Design Edit

After the content and copy edit it is time for design edit. Design edit is the step before it goes to the printer. At this point, typestyle is chosen, page margins and chapter headings are reviewed to make certain chapters flow smoothly. At this stage, go through the book and indicate charts, chapter headings, subheadings,

Don't delay,
start writing today.

– Cuttie W. Bacon, III

italic, bold, and any other designs that you want for your final copy. Make certain that the design looks like the final product you want. You are finally ready to put your manuscript in the hands of a printer. However, it is never too late to spell check and double check each edit before sending your manuscript to the printer. The closer your manuscript is to perfect, the quicker you can move to your final product.

It is common for new authors to be preoccupied with producing the perfect book. This preoccupation with perfection can be a hindrance when completing a final manuscript.

After you have completed your 3-Step Editing Process, set a deadline to submit your manuscript for printing. Have your final copy checked before submitting it to the printer. Should anyone be kind enough to find one or two mistakes, assure them that you will make corrections in the second printing of your book and don't worry about it.

Make big decisions about your book with your heart.

Make little decisions about your book with your head.

– Cuttie W. Bacon, III

Features that Sell Books

Many new authors sometimes get excited in writing their book and overlook one of the primary reasons for writing a book is to sell it. In my opinion the number one feature of a book that should be considered is the book cover. I've realized for many years and we have heard the quotation, "You can't judge a book by its cover," but the cover of a book can be the most important feature in how well it sells. Most consumers, when trying to make a decision to buy a book, spend less than two minutes in looking at the book and making a decision to buy. The cover of the book including the spine and the back cover are crucially important to the sale. In most bookstores today, a consumer sees the spine before the cover. It is truly important to have an attractive spine that commands the attention of the consumer. Only then will a person take the time to look at the front and back of the book. The spine gets the book selected off the shelf. The front and back cover must then support the spine of the book when the consumer is browsing the shelves. After the cover, the spine, and the exterior design of the book, the table of contents, the number of pages, and the price will also contribute to the sale of the book.

Additional Features that Sell Books

Title of the Book. Titles influence the sale of books. Books that meet an everyday need, books that have emotional titles, and books that have the ability to provoke curiosity and emotions help sales. Remember titles of books cannot be copyrighted. You can use any title you want for your book as long as it isn't a trademark.

A very simple principle in developing a title for your book is to let the reader know how the book will benefit him and what the book will do for him if he reads it. For example, "How to always win an argument."

Title. The title helps the reader clearly and quickly decide what the book will do for him and may also address a need the reader has. It is perfectly acceptable to give emotional titles to your book that quickly grabs the attention of consumers.

Subject. Try to find new and exciting subjects that are not already on the shelves. Also look for subjects that provide a service or need for consumers. Nine out of ten American consumers face problems with credit and spending. "How to" subjects that tell consumers how to charge, how to save, and how not to become overwhelmed with credit cards are fresh and also serve a need.

Table of Contents. Table of Contents help sell books. The Table of Contents should be colorful, attractive and should quickly show the browser information on what they will get from the book. The Table of Contents gives a clear look at what is in the book. An author needs to make certain that a reader can quickly access what the book offers. The Table of Contents should be presented in 2 or less pages so that the reader can quickly make a decision about whether or not they want to buy the book for its content.

Book Design. The content design of a book can assist in selling the book. Although most readers only spend a few seconds thumbing through a book before they buy it, the more professional in appearance, the easier it is for the reader to decide that he or she is going to purchase the book. In preparing your book, (Content Design) if you do not have a person who is skillful in designing the content, you can use the services of a consultant. Many times your printing company will assist you in giving a professional design to your book.

Reviews. Many writers use part of the back of their book or the front page of their book to list reviews of their publications. Having several reviews by highly respected people in the field, celebrities, talk show host

"You can't judge a book by its cover," but the cover of a book can be the most important feature in how well it sells.

– Cuttie W. Bacon, III

and people with considerable notoriety can assist in selling your book. Many readers look for reviews and respect the opinions of noted people in the field, celebrities, and other people of notoriety.

Using all of the above to sell your book, and making certain that you put your book in as many hands as possible such as libraries, book stores, and other outlets will enhance the sale of your book and the circulation and success of your book.

How to Present Yourself as a Professional Writer

Now that you are about to publish your book, you will never be the same after this experience. So, never underestimate yourself from this point on.

Adopt a 24-hour positive attitude. Develop a genuine smile if you don't have one because when you smile the world smiles with you. Start accepting compliments graciously. When someone tells you have a great book, thank them with a smile and tell them that you greatly appreciate the compliment. Never say, "It's nothing" or "I wrote it in just 6 hours." When someone asks you if you are a writer, graciously say, "Yes." Keep 3 or 4 speeches ready and be prepared to speak on your book on short notice. Keep plenty of your products on hand and always be happy to autograph your book.

Everyone admires a writer.

– Cuttie W. Bacon, III

CHAPTER 7

Do's and Don'ts for a Successful Book

Do's for a Successful Book

There are many rules and recommendations for publishing and promoting a book. First and most importantly is the front, back and the spine. The cover of your book is extremely important because that is the way books are sold. There are numerous things that will influence a person to make a decision to buy a book. The most important factor in influencing a person to buy a book is clearly the cover. In the bookstore, consumers do not have time to read your book. In many instances the consumer will give a book less than five seconds of their time. The cover of the book is the main attraction. The cover will assist a consumer in attaching himself to the book. Having a feeling for the book will give a hint to the reader what the book is all about.

Do Position Yourself to Make Money

1. Get yourself an e-mail address. A web-site is even better.
2. Get a toll free number. (It only costs $12.00 to get started.) This allows people to access you easily.

3. Get a Post Office Box. Use it for all of your correspondence.

4. Develop an order blank. List your book and any other items that you have to sell.

5. Order your Library of Congress Number and your list of ISBN numbers right away. It may take 6 - 8 weeks to receive them.

Library of Congress Number
Library of Congress Catalog Numbers
Application form 607-7
202-707-6372.

ISBN Number
International Standard Book Numbering Agency
121 Chanlon Road
New Providence, NJ 079474
800-521-8110

Copyright Your Book
Register of Copyrights
Library of Congress
Washington, DC 20559-6000
Form TX

Note: Copyright information is explained in detail in Chapter 11.

In summary, there is power in a cover. In the bookstore it is the spine that gets the book removed from the shelf. The second most influential part of the book after a consumer takes it from the shelf is the interior design. Many consumers will quickly read a few lines or paragraphs of the book to see what the quality of the book is. Many will review the table of contents, scan it and check the price and how thick the book is. All the above things play a part in assisting a consumer to make a decision to buy a book. A consumer making a decision usually makes a rather quick decision. As a publisher the time you spend designing the cover and the spine of your book is time well spent.

Don'ts for a Successful Book

Don't design your book cover or spine unless you are a graphic artist and have extensive experience in designing covers that are successful sellers. Don't publish obsolete, over published and dead topics. For example, I was at the bookstore the other day and counted 51 different books on various methods on how to play golf.

Don't allow the person to edit your book who has little experience in editing successful books. Having correct grammar, spelling, sentence structure and vocabulary is important. A book that looks professional will sell.

Don't publish a book and leave off bar codes. Many larger bookstores will not stock books that do not have bar codes. Don't publish books with copyrights that are too old. Many bookstores and consumers do not want books that do not have a current copyright date. Don't attempt to write or publish a book on a subject that you are not familiar with. Write through education or experiences.

*One man's junk may be
another man's treasure.*

– Cuttie W. Bacon, III

CHAPTER 8

A Marketing Plan for Your Book

There are numerous ways to market a self-published book. I have experienced everything from a self-publisher standing on the corner selling his book, or a paper man standing on the corner selling newspapers and as elaborate as a caviar champagne book signing at a fabulous downtown hotel. Here are five approaches that have worked best for me in selling my book:

Being a national and international professional speaker and selling my books at speaking engagements have been some of the most successful ways that I have been able to sell and market my products.

I have noticed that in speaking to groups of people, particularly large groups, there is a relationship formed with them that at the end of the speech, many in the audience appear to want to take home a piece of what I said, my philosophy, and something related to me. It appears that people believe that my book is a part of me that they want to keep. In selling books after a speech, I simply position a table at the back of the room or outside the room, generally with one person to assist me in collecting the money while I personally autograph every book that is sold after my speeches. People also like a personally signed book from the author and to meet, greet and shake your hand after the speech. For professional speakers, this can be a fantastic way to supplement your income. Sometimes you can experience earning more from your book than from the speaking engagement.

A second successful way of selling books is participating in conferences and seminars. Sometimes participating only as a panel member and positioning your books in the back of the room can have the same or similar effect as being a keynote speaker and giving a major speech. Again, people will want to keep part of you and the part you want them to have is a copy of your book.

A third way that has been very successful for me is selling books at bazaars and festivals where vendors are common and where there are a variety of products available for sale to large groups interested in spending money. Bazaars and similar festivals give you an opportunity to meet and greet large numbers of people to sign and autograph your book and to be able to tell people about the content of your book. It is also an excellent way to network and find other avenues for the sale of your book.

Churches, temples and other religious institutions are other excellent ways to sell your book. Speaking to groups at religious institutions of 300 or more can generate some of the same reactions that you get when speaking at conferences and being a keynote speaker.

Never forget to avail yourself to personally sign all books purchased. There is something magical about having a newly purchased book signed by the author of the book. Personally presenting your book to small store owners and large store owners and convincing them that they should stock your book can be an excellent and direct way of getting your book on the shelf in local and national bookstores.

In addition to the above marketing possibilities for your book, there are national exclusive distributors, sales reps, independent sales reps, wholesalers, jobbers, catalogs sales, book clubs, wholesale clubs, and numerous other possibilities of marketing and selling your book. The method you use is personal preference that works well for you. Remember, as a self-publisher you have the highest potential for earning money on your book because you do not have a middleman. Limiting the use of middlemen will allow you a greater return and more control on the selling of the book.

Remember
You have only just begun.

– Cuttie W. Bacon, IV

CHAPTER 9

If You Can Write a Speech, You Can Write a Book

Frequently we hear if you've got a speech, you've got a book. I would take that statement a step further and say if you have an excellent speech, you have the possibility of an excellent book. Well known and powerful speakers like Dr. Martin Luther King, Jr. went to great lengths and spent considerable time outlining, developing and putting together a speech. My recommendation is to first tell the audience what you are going to talk about. The beginning of the book should explain to the reader what you are going to tell them. The middle should be the content. The end should be the conclusion and the restating of what you told them. Quotes are important in a speech. They can also be used very well in a book. The start of speeches can begin with facts. I recommend that you start a speech with a first draft, revise it to an intermediate draft, and end it with a final draft. In writing a book from a speech I would recommend the same approach. A good speech outline can be converted into a book.

A good speech outline can be converted into a book.

– Cuttie W. Bacon, III

A Must to Remember When Writing Your Book

Always be truthful with what you are writing about. You need to love what you are writing about and you need to share it colorfully. Writing books represents one of the more credible things you can do. Writing books can also be about profit. Many people earn millions of dollars writing books. However, that should not be your only motivation.

Do not become preoccupied with whether or not your spelling, grammar, or syntax is perfect. Remember you have probably been led to believe those were reasons why you never wrote your book. You can hire a person to edit every word you write. Computers have grammar check, spell check and punctuation check, or any check that you need.

Remember the topic of your book is something you know a great deal about. If it is about you, you already know more about you than anyone else in the world!

We live in the information age today. Thousands of books are being published every week. You will NEVER know everything there is to be known about ANY subject. So go for it!

If you can write a great speech,
You can write a great book.

– Cuttie W. Bacon, III

CHAPTER 10

Self-Publishing

Self-publishing can be a highly successful way of publishing your book. There is a generally accepted myth that the Library of Congress questions self published books and that bookstores won't carry self published books. The truth of the matter is the Library of Congress may question self-published books using your individual name as the publishing company, but the solution to this problem is creating a professional sounding publisher's name. The professional name of your company should be on the par with names like Harper and Row, Beacon Press, Tandem Publishing and others. Using professional names will eliminate any questions about you as an individual publishing your own book. Self-publishing will allow you to realize a considerably larger portion of the selling price of your book than if you used an established publisher. Large publishers may put up the money to promote and advertise your book and pay your expenses of traveling across the country to do book signings. Many writers have had the experience of large companies paying for the promotion, travel, and all expenses to get the books sold. However, after subtracting the expenses to pro-

———

A writer directly selling his own book can realize 75% and more of the selling price of the book.

– Cuttie W. Bacon, III

———

mote the books, some writers have realized only 10% and an even lower portion of the retail selling price. A writer directly selling his own book can realize 75% and more of the selling price of the book. A writer distributing his or her own book can receive 30 or more percent of the selling price of the book by directly distributing them to bookstores. For these and numerous other reasons it is wise to publish and sell your own book to allow yourself a higher income from your work.

Another advantage of self-publishing is that you can have 100% control of the content of your book rather than allowing a publisher to delete or add what they would like.

Lastly, the sooner your manuscript is ready for press, the sooner you can publish your book. Some publishing companies may take years to publish your book. You can self-publish it in a month or two.

You can't pay someone to write from your heart. YOU must write from your heart.

— Cuttie W. Bacon, III

CHAPTER 11

Copyright Notices, Registration

To avoid copyright infringement, you must understand the basics of copyright law, what copyrights protect, and how long copyrights last.

Copyright Registration

The registration process is fairly simple. The fee is not exorbitant, just $20.

There are two primary reasons to register your work by copyright: (1) for statutory damages, and (2) the ability to sue.

You cannot sue, however, anyone for infringing your copyright until you have registered your work with the Copyright Office. If you register your work within three months from the date of first publication, you can collect statutory damages from the infringer.

Copyright Notice

It is customary to attach a copyright notice on copyrighted material to be eligible for certain types of damages.

There are five basic elements of a copyright notice. They include:

- The copyright symbol

- The term "Copyright"

- The year of the copyright

- The name of the copyright holder

- The phrase "All rights reserved

Example:

Copyright © 2000 Cuttie W. Bacon
All Rights Reserved

The term "Copyright" is not required in the copyright notice. However, it should be noted that the term "Copyright" may now be used in lieu of the © Copyright Symbol in the United States.

Note: The © is generally the standard identifier of a Copyright Notice.

What Copyrights Do Not Protect

Copyright protects expression. An original expression is eligible for copyright protection as soon as it is fixed in its final form. However, not everything is eligible for copyright. These are examples of items that are not eligible for copyright protection:

- Titles

- Names

- Short phrases

- Blank forms

- Ideas

ISBN Number

ISBN numbers can be obtained from RR Broker, 121 Chanlon Road, New Providence, New Jersey 07974. You can purchase 20 numbers for approximately $200 and have numbers to cover the next twenty books that you publish.

SAN Numbers

SAN means Standard Address Number. The Standard Address Number is useful in assisting people who are interested in locating you to quickly look up your number and check your name and address. Having a SAN Number will assist you in appearing to be a larger publisher. You can obtain this number by requesting it when you order your ISBN Number.

*It is difficult to write a book
without the help of
other people.*

– Cuttie W. Bacon, III

CHAPTER 12

One Big Step Left

You need to find a graphic person who understands how to produce a book. The person will be one who can do magic with words and one who can save you money when you go to the printer. When you call my 800 number I will supply you with a pamphlet of all the steps to getting your final product on the bookshelf. You can call at 1-800-955-9934.

Get Started, Don't Proscrastinate

I've told you more than enough to write your book. Call my 800 number for my pamphlet if you need information on getting your book printed, and help on producing audio tapes of your book. The number is 1-800-955-9934.

Words From the Author

Congratulations on purchasing this book. This system has worked for me in writing several books and I am sure it will work for you. I hope you will use this book and tell your friends to obtain a copy. Also you may want to use it as a gift. Each time I mention my book, whether I am at a party, on a plane or at a book signing, people have said to me that they would like to have this type of book.

I have only one request of you after you publish your book. Please share at least one copy of it with me so I can have it on my bookshelf and brag that I assisted you in writing and publishing your book.

Words are very powerful. Remember to use them wisely in your book. Writing a book with powerful words makes you a powerful person.

Thank you.

The Author's Brag Page

Cuttie Bacon, III was born in Western Kentucky and lived the first four years of his life on a farm where his father was a farmer. At an early age his parents moved to Louisville, Kentucky where he graduated from Central High School. He later graduated from Kentucky State University in nearby Frankfort receiving his Bachelors degree in Business Administration. After graduation, he moved to Chicago where he earned a Master's Degree at Loyola University and a Ph.D. at Northwestern University in Evanston, Illinois.

Dr. Bacon has taught at Northwestern University, Mundelein College and Governors State University. He has led numerous seminars over the past 10 years. His career which began as a public school teacher in Chicago Public Schools ultimately culminated in positions as Principal and Superintendent of Schools in the Southern Suburbs of Chicago. Cuttie is an active member of the Chicago Chapter of the National Association of African American Speakers. He frequently speaks on "How to Live the Good Life," "Effective Classroom Management and School Violence," "Charter Schools: A Threat to Public Education?"

He is the father of two adult children: Cutia and Cuttie IV, and the grandfather of four girls: Candace Joi, Christine Alexis, Marya Olivia and Cutia Jacqueline.

Cuttie is an entertaining speaker and often recounts stories which illustrate the humorous side of primary, secondary and higher education.

Cuttie consistently speaks on developing a prosperity conscious. Call Dr. Knose seminars; 1-800-955-9934.

Seminar to Start Your Book

Now that you have read the book and you need a little more information, stimulation and motivation, gather 20 people or more together and call Dr. Knose seminars. I will come in and give you and your group a book writing seminar, get you started and have you laughing all the way. Just call 1-800-955-9934.

Other Products to Order by Dr. Bacon

- How to Teach Kids to be Millionaires

- How to Write Your Own Book Audio Tapes

- How to Teach Kids to be Millionaires Post Cards

Afterwords

Now that you have read my book on how to write your own book, don't procrastinate. GET STARTED TODAY! Remember, if you want to write your book within 30 days, start typing at least 3 single spaced pages a day and in 30 days you will have your first rough draft.

Most of us have an awful lot of information to share with people and the world. Please do not cheat people any longer. Put those experiences in a book and share them with the world.

Best of success in your book!

Bibliography

Poynter, Dan. *Write and Grow Rich.* Santa Barbara: Para Publishing, 1999

Kozak, Ellen M. *Every Writer's Guide to Copyright and Publishing Law.* New York: Henry Holt and Company, Inc., 1990

Brodie, Deborah. *Writing Changes Everything.* New York: St. Martin's Press. 1997

Cardoza, Avery. *The Complete Guide to Successful Publishing.* New York: Cardoza Publishing, 1995

Winget, Larry. *How to Write a Book One Page at a Time.* Tulsa: Win Publications, 1996

Ryan, Margaret. *How to Give a Speech.* New York: Franklin Watts, 1994

Page, Susan. *The Shortest Distance Between You and a Published Book.* New York: Broadway Books, 1997

Smith, Ronald Ted. *Book Publishing Encyclopedia.* Sarasota: Book World Press, 1996

Order Information

To order more copies of this book or receive other products by Cuttie W. Bacon III, Ph.D., contact Dr. Bacon by calling toll free 1-800-955-9934, or write him at P.O. Box 81465, Chicago, IL 60681, or email at Cuttie3@compuserve.com. How to Write Your Own Book is a trademark of Dr. Knose Publications, Dr. Knose Seminars and Cuttie W. Bacon, III.

* * * * *

To have Dr. Bacon speak to your organization
or to order any of his other products contact:

Dr. Knose Seminars:

Call 1-800-955-9934

or write him at

P.O. Box 81465
Chicago, IL 60681

or e-mail at

Cuttie3@compuserve.com

Dr. Bacon will be happy to provide personal consultation to assist you with getting started with your first book and with planning future books thereafter. For more information:

Call
1-800-955-9934
or e-mail at
Cuttie3@compuserve.com

*Additional help is
only a phone call away.*